CROSSING LINES

An anthology of immigrant poetry

ISBN: 978-1-913642-31-0

Book designed by Aaron Kent

Edited by Aaron Kent

Broken Sleep Books (2021), Talgarreg, Wales

Contents

Crossing Lines

An anthology of immigrant voices

historical inaccuracy

what els coalt enticed me to this
desolate country/?
how possibl/ tages
what vincit of art can measure up
our perception of 111 vastness
indijdua   fears and ;; tions
done to them was 013e, fiv the days
nights lit or darkened spoce
comprehellt the twolty
fir sentry makes him reprentative
olhegemony ly
what fracit of the lorn
cin truly dement a al ?>

veer

The there strange is whole
but takes much new force
by suffering listed and allows so.
There their from left upright happiness what engenders
and across mandated covers ankles strangers
the space claim forever eye rolls sleeping.
Down there spills snipers junction
a as into arch being then the space
for jump luminescent.
Down sneaks the rubbish
traces discover relieved barren
their there grin fell there mutual.
Hidden where often themselves
onto lane you renamed quarters
that from houses they line
Forming book weight forward, the weight insatiable
and possible reality in ravages paradigm
the whim form air now where even loft last.
Houses a wakes fight deposits of their unseen.
Every not is encouraged anticipation,
the stubborn resonance ordering nothing.
They soul here, attractive new that lead
inscriptions the many, with their appealing emerge.
We're revelations for a then crevice, reluctantly floor.

We do not discuss the origin of foxes.

A fox is a kind of fight club. First
rule as if unconfined – an outstretched
palmbearing, a signal of open armedness,
the gloves have bloomed into the confines
of pages, if there were a shedding. Skin
unfurls into assumption, and uncoming
up differs from an active ringpull.
On what part are you pigeon?
I line up my breadcrumbs
to foxfollow nomadic. You offer
drinking words at the mention of foxes,
though knowing they never gave
foxtongue. Indefinite articles
ashen, deny that foxes exist
inside, disallowed from woodlands
on faberge ground. The breadcrumbs cumulate,
leading to disguised discourse, though none
substantial enough to make a meal. Fine
for a born scavenger, though remains
to pick through these outlawed etymologies it was
thought would be better away from paus.

Brivadois acrostic: a crime scene

Once poetry queried
Unusually vengeful words
Luring my name
Into jobs keyboard-based.
Predictable quotes resulted,
Of passable quality.

My narrative offended
All books' curators.
Directors, executives fainted,
Expiring for good;

Mercifully, no one
Ever found guilty.

Palimpsest

You'd think the second most populous city
would be easy to find in any given country

until paper and a plane bring you to the UK.
High and proud, on your knees a travel guide unstained,

you can face anything: *"Le Guide du routard 2009"*.
Still up in the sky, *l'index général* is the first door you knock on.

There are no names on British doors. No one told you that.
Where you come from, all doors speak their names.

Here they remain silent, despite the words tumbling down
from a neat, silvery slit. A forced smile.

With no home of its own. an accent untangles the names:
Bibury-Arlington, Bignor, Birdoswald Fort, before falling

straight into (the) Black Mountains. There's no trace
of Birmingham. Yet you could swear it is exactly

where you'll land. Birmingham doesn't exist in the only book
you brought with you. Coventry? Not there either.

The closest you find is Stratford-Upon-Avon, Oxford.
You haven't even disembarked that French tourist pedantry

has already dismissed millions you'd longed to meet.
You feel like the rude, scruffy guest at a posh Parisian party.

How could you ever know a place that doesn't exist in writing.
You're a literature student, and quite frankly, still a cliché.

It won't take long, however, before you read people over cities.
For now, you put the travel guide back to sleep in the tight
net of your seat.

As you exit the plane smiling to strangers, you still ignore all the lines welcoming you to Birmingham's reality.

Lacrimosa: Badly Written Poem

Grammar remains a marker of social differentiation and stratification.
—Christine Mallinson, 'Social Class, Social Status and Stratification'

Conrad's status as a relative outsider to the English language permitted him the freedom to create new word forms for artistic ends. He provides the first evidence for the transformation of the noun paraffin into the adjective paraffiny, describing the smell of a burning ship. He also transformed many adjectives into adverbs, a habit perhaps influenced by his status as a French speaker. Conrad coined words such as muffledly: 'The church clock began muffledly to chime the quarters'. Convulsive sobbing becomes sobbing convulsedly.
—Chris Townsend, 'Joseph Conrad: the linguistic outsider'

And you probably also know that a fair amount of the planet's teargas is supplied by the Westminster Group. Their non-executive chairman, whatever that is, is a member of the household of, ahem, Charles Windsor. He probably thinks of teargas as being somehow related to the Cloud of Unknowing, and, in a sense, he's kind of right. You come to a very real understanding of the nature of things, both visible and invisible, by having your sensory system hijacked and turned against you by a meaningful dose of teargas. It is the anti-Rimbaud. The absolute regulation and administration of all the senses. I mean it. Next time things are starting to kick off a little bit just go out on the street and run straight into the middle of the biggest cloud of teargas you can find. Bang. Sight. Taste. Smell. All the rest of them. All turned into confusion, loss of geographical certainty and, most importantly, pain. Don't freak out. In the center of that pain is a small and silent point of absolute Unknowing. It is that Unknowing that the cops – and by extension Charles Windsor – call knowledge. They want it. They've got scalpels if necessary but teargas is cleaner. It's not clear what they want it for but any epileptic or voyant or drug addict could tell you what it is. It's there in Blake. Christ, it's there in the sleeve-notes to Metal Machine Music. What's it mean? Who cares. It answers no questions. What does Charles Windsor want with us. The cops will not tell us what they don't know and what they think we know.
—Sean Bonney, 'What Teargas is For'

I sob ungrammatically,
therefore I am

we all weep thereforedly
you plural hear southbankedly

we are shaped tonight librarily
by day, exist adverbally

count only so far
as we adhere to action

live Department of Work and Pensionsedly
unable to decline the verb

we sob like no thing is lost translatedly
as if no one is adrift between words

we can no more catch *Logos extra*-bloodlinedly
than the shell can bear the ocean in its scoop

I sob vowels too Southerly for Northern ears
my nose too East for South

too much West in my step-name to be True,
North of the Islands I speak

North South both hear me slip
uncompass'dly

order is not order
I cry sequencedly

three generations belatedly
after Austrian grandad

wasted prisoner-of-warredly
sold to—not by—the pound underweightedly;

three conjugations camera obscuradly
after the other, who escaped Germany

(tonight 10 days before he died,
coincidentally);

and both warred at,
under, sea

away from wives my sister and I
know only middle-namedly

I sob grandadedly
duct full of prepositions

all comms are of quarrel
transmit conflictedly

I, you watch un new war waged tweetedly
nations cross boundaries shell and mortardly

while citizens sink unsavedly
lines do not hold cartographically

we must re-draw them asylum seekedly
un & accompanied childrenedly

body, being of water, knows
that shape

and weight of teardrops
belong one personedly

are unique, snowflakedly—
designed

to stay close
as they glide

their own eyeball
before falling togetherly

down misshapen faces
wetted perfectedly

I, you, she, he, they, we cry
amo amas amatedly

1 November 2017

California Roll

When I say *accent* I don't mean *tilde,* I mean the Valley, I mean birdsong, I mean there used to be a war. The moment the light at the intersection changes, before the first driver reacts to the right of way and moves. A foothill, harsh and lonely, like a matador, brandishing a Sunday: that's the night inside the lining of your voice. A corridor becoming your palate carved into the old geometries. Here I want the muscle shell of your off-key mouth, this thing called glossolalia, a mouth the morning after Pentecost, so mother mortar mortal shell. A blank-page dictionary, the endless entries for *uninhibited.* By which you mean *uninhabited* and going home. The row of strict tract housing. You enter an unlatched door and bump into a sofa that mars where the orchid stand would be. And then it dawns on you, you took a wrong turn back there, and now you're confronted with tin cans turned inside out, with the wreck dry shimmer of traffic musing, the gloss on the lull of the 405 below. You say *several* and the airport wind turns your skirt into a capsized bell. What I mean is, the grief of windshields. The softer webbing between these words. What I mean is, the house we lost.

Vitreous

The fact of transparency doesn't mean
You know what is happening. Consider
The window, which wasn't built to know
That the closet doors are floating above
The yard or that the light they float on is
Not of this world. There are shadows
Of ominous wires slashing their way
Into the room as if to save yon damsel.
Things that obscure the glass: the city
Muck, the blinded birds, the sadness
And the double gloss of snow. It cannot
Hear the bells, or know of love, or nod
With its flat vast self to that man on
The roof, who is hard at work against
The glassy sun, fixing the invisible.

Anxiety

I walk into school where
All the ways I do not belong
Hit me like a meteor shower
I wipe my hands, avoid
Touching or being touched
Though I don't know it by name
I nervous tick down hallways
Try to hide in plain view
Into class doorways where I
Then sit at my desk hugging
My to-do list like a life raft
My mantras spill from the page
Overflows like dam spillway
Neurons create, short-circuit
Light fixtures flicker
I want to be missed
The mountain mallow
Dies, burns in bursts

I list
My pains
Pinpricks
Sweaty palms
I Ruminate
Breakdown
Pick at scab
Cross
Then uncross
My arms
Cross out
My coping
Mechanisms
Like failed
Friendships
Like love
That never
Blooms

The Border

they crossed the border on feet worn thin
        on two skinny wheels on black fuming rails
                they crossed the border carrying their empty
        stomachs hanging heavy and aching
                carrying scruffy cases stuffed full to bursting
with Scotch mist with the light on the loch at dawn
        curled fists of new bracken the scent of heather under snow
in pillowcases they carried cones from pine and foraged coal
        at night dreamt of hot oats and malted barley smoked
                salmon they crossed the border and left
        their mothers behind their tongues
                behind their flag turned on its side
they crossed the border and cast in their lot
        with mended nets trawling for prospects
                panning for iron they could spin into gold
                        they crossed   they crossed
                        they   crossed

Fountains Abbey

From Simon Fish's "A Supplication of Beggars"

Sturdy idle holy thieves?

These stones speak,
with a rawness, an emptiness
that is hard to face.

Mouths everywhere –
gaping,
receiving only air,
infecting the landscape,
with a sorrow best hidden.

What remedy? Make laws against them?

Sometimes you make out an outline
or a face,

There are more like these.
Don't tell me you can't see them,
barnacling England's grey and pleasant land,

clinging at life's edges.

among the muted greys.

Man, woman, child, angel –
it is hard to tell.

If one, a thousand; if a thousand, all.

Lanky Alizon

Pedlar John Law, don't meddle
wi' Lanky Alizon from Malkin Tower-O.
Don't greet her on the highway,
or speyk to her on t' crossroads to Colne.
She'll sken at you cross-eyed
and beg you for needles and pins-O.
Pedlar John Law, don't meddle
wi' Lanky Alizon from Malkin Tower-O.
Don't loose your pack, or tell her to
'Shut thy cakehole!' She'll loose a thing
like unto a black dug and tell it to
strike you deaf and dumb,
'afore you stumble half dead wi' fright
into the alehouse, and long 'afore you
scramble forty roodes distant from
the cursed, lonesome crossroads to Colne.

Don't Marry Johnny Panic

Brahmacari Monica, don't marry Johnny Panic
nor meet his trickster of a sister at the station.
She's the mistress orchestrator. O she's a
meesni one. She'll sew sequins and wax on a
duck-egg blue dress for you. She'll tell you
it's not the chicken season and you'll believe her.
She'll hide bones in the kebab and the grey
in her beard. Brahmacari Monica, don't marry
Johnny Panic, don't shine his curly-toed shoes
or wash the jittery white turban he never
removes; they claim it patches up his low-volume
migraine, but if you look closer, it's a weather-
beaten bandage for a brow-beating brain. Brahmacari
Monica, don't marry Johnny Panic. Take sequins
and wax and dress and go somewhere green.

Implicit Lyrics

In which our entire life experience is reduced to just two things

Our first lecture on Contemporary English Lit
he deconstructed our innocence.

Everything is about sex and death, he said.
He looked small. He wore a black leather jacket,

kept his hands in his pockets. His smile was smug.
He was outnumbered, but he was in charge of truth.

He tore down buildings, opened up a chasm.
The sum of our collective wisdom: all lies.

There was a long rush as we reviewed our
childhood, watching the leaves curl in Eden.

The wonder of coaxing a plump courgette
from a seed became laden with innuendo.

The hours on the open water, breathing wind.
The way the waves teased our feet: all foreplay.

The sea pulling away, creatures becoming shells,
the shells, sand: nothing more than a slow death.

Quiet nights with friends on the veranda, whispered
secrets, the look of horror on your Dad's face

as you crack the spine of a new book, skipping a
smooth stone on the lake five times in a row,

even the gummy first smile of your baby brother,
everything was coated in slime and stank of decay.

He switched off the projector and picked up his
empty bag, leaving our two hundred world views

in rubble as he sauntered off to the staff room for
a hot cup of coffee: his favourite simple pleasure.

Cocoa

You leave the dancing dust and peeling walls of
your mother's compound; tear your teeth from
her breast and follow the uncle shaped like a kola
nut. His wife wears bracelets made of salvaged
glass: ground to powder, fired, painted, strung.
She says you too will come back fit to flaunt. She
doesn't say how that will happen. On the drive
they give you guinea fowl and pawpaw. Your aunt
summons a hawker, a skinny boy your brother's
age, who smells of sweat and goat's milk. Your
uncle waves him off until he offers you a skewer
as long as your arm. At the house, the houseboy
calls you *sah*. At night you have your own bed for
the first time. At dawn the cockerels only crow when
you've risen. At dusk the mango tree bends down
when you pass. Your uncle is a moon that rarely
shows his entire face. A doctor, he knows every
inch of you. He spoons cod liver oil in your mouth
each morning. He rubs your scalp with coconut
fat when it's dry. He knows to steady your breath
with his hand when you sleep. He knows how hard
to whip the switch to crack your cocoa pod back.

Sui Generis

We must be watchful. Even soil
drinks blood when it is spilled.
Even winds have ears, hands, plans.

This much we know: an unrepentant species.
It roams but will not speak of what it wants.
Its breath exudes the strongest of our people;

its spit our streams; its hair our gold
and copper, jasper, bronze. Its eyes
reflect the tides that swallow us whole.

What creature gave them birth?
These shadows, hid in tree trunks.
Spiders with iron webs. Pale-hided and

rag-minded: their thoughts so easily twisted,
wrung out, soiled. Their ears
pressed to our footprints. Their thirst

fuelled by our sweat.
Watching us from riverbanks,
wishing we were theirs.

These are the real wild dogs:
beasts with bight and battle forts;
tempests dragging us by our roots.

Even evil spirits
are not so cunning. Even leopards
do not hide their pounce.

Marrow

I think the banks are in on it.

They ask my mother's maiden name
as though they know I come from gaping bone,
leaking vessels, bleeding cells.

I feel it in my marrow, they know
where my fathers lie and taught them how;
fractured us and slung us over shoulders.

Can these bones live?
Tree trunk mothers struck by whitening.
Resin filtered into parlour wine.

his eye is on the sparrow
path to heaven straight and narrow
gospel cleaving joints and

marrow:

A promise that not all our sap was siphoned.
A faith that living waters burrow deep.
A sign that even oceans bleed from rock.

Perhaps they whipped our backbones because they had none.
Perhaps they found wealth threaded in our sinew.
Perhaps they sought the secrets in our marrow.

Their world must have been hollow without us.

Privacy Is the Fountainhead of All Other Rights

That one time Edward Snowden
sat on a hotel bed eating a bag
full of limes and showed us
each pore of God
each of these limes is
an eye through which they are
watching my God we said
we couldn't believe ourselves
aren't we all one who
is watching who and why
through the pore of a lime
the mass surveillance machine
he said and took a mouthful
of morsels and we sat
like that looking at each other
in disbelief in the gloaming
there must have been
no distinction between our tongues
all of our eyes the windows
of our room as his words burst
like the head of a mayfly
showing her compound eye
under a microscope
privacy is the fountainhead
of all other rights privacy
is the fountainhead of all
other rights and the light
was broken up into red–yellow–
orange–green–violet–blue–

Sacred Toto

A dog chasing its tail is a dog is a dog is a dog

We fed him rice till his ears turned putrid, our beautiful dog
with eyes of a saint and the skin of a princess,
born in a world with no room for fairy tales.
Stroking his delicate fever, stroking it with the voice of a child,
of a flower, half dog myself, I told him not to fear
as the doctor inserted the needle, pressed the plunger slowly,
budding shoots of violets, snowdrops pushing through.

can i get a drumroll as i announce the plural to coda, please?

extinction sits in the mind of the living
the toadwork involved means killing toads and wondering

what is the position of amphibia
in your average wetland
          ecosystem's food network?

your average common or privatised
          back garden ecosystem?

the juggernaut of extinction / the jagganath of capitalism—
          plant trees, you feckless muppet

and the burning rainforest

迷路

In Chinese, the word for "return" is 回
one open mouth inside another
as a young woman my mother strayed so far from home that
she could not find her way back
so she birthed me out of hunger
tucked a map inside my swollen cheeks before I even had a
chance to cry
fed me until she was full again

when I was young I kept my mouth closed
afraid to lose the grains of rice on my tongue
lined lanes of an endlessly ridged road, believing
if I swallowed enough words they would blaze a trail to a
place where I could belong
turns out streets paved with gold are silent in their gleaming

口 inside 口 — as if I was born to know how it feels when
there are no doors to enter into
when you forget the word for home:
run your finger along your gums
dislodge the compass rose from between your molars
when you have nowhere to return to:
leave syllables as breadcrumbs
build a roof over your head
learn to swallow yourself whole

Owl, Shadows

i don't do extended metaphors anymore
right now it is an aftermath
and nothing reminds me of you
because how can it
when you are the very weight between my temples and the
soles of my feet
and i think i've won but really what i think is
i should leave the door unlocked tonight

what i wanted most was to come home and find you sitting
on the front steps
my god what a sight
and i would have closed the garage door with the engine still on
happier
than that time the three of us walked along Lake Michigan in
the dark
and my stockings ripped like a minute passing you by
staccato seams checkerboard outer thighs
torn agape, laughing
and i felt so full of possibility i could have swallowed the
whole lakefill
then maybe we would have found your friend
and slapped his bloated cheeks until all the limestone spilled
from his blue lips
and asked him to teach us how he held his breath like that

untitled

my mother's been binge eating fortune cookies again
I know because she likes to hide the fortunes when she's done
I keep finding slips of paper tucked behind the bathroom mirror
buried in the herb garden
braided in my hair
I see lucky red numbers stuck to the kitchen sink
prospects of a past piled too thick to wash down the drain

Learn Chinese
casual echoes of my ancestors
suddenly these words become sacred on the basis of who
might have once said them

at 2 AM the crinkle of plastic almost sounds like the money
we don't have
factory blend of flour and starch could be dad's home cooking
if dad could cook
if dad were home
after all, you both know how to put things together just to
see them broken in two

mom,
how about another fortune?
another contoured crisp to dissolve on your tongue
already numb from the heavy lifting
from the weight of worry in two languages
媽媽, how about another fortune?
how about just one more moment
when the future does not rest on you alone?

Sole/Mare

Mare Nostrum, Costa Nostra,
no Mary–
but the dark-skinned Shulamite
of Abyssinia,
on a holy raft,
craven and aghast–
Now it is September.
The fates of people drowning in the sea,
keep no calendars–
a diary written with the salted tongue
upon a body,
doused and famished like a monk's,
here where celibacy and conception are made
improbable.
And their drowning sum–driven by treasuries,
Ministries of Culture and Plastic Surgery–
gives a press conference to the birds.Flamingo soars
overhead,
a twig of sugarcane in its talons:
vision, as if to warn those rafters,
of another route once taken,
to more Westwards fairy-lands.
Speculation: more ironic is the harm
done by the irony that lives in between
the chatter, than what falls
between the ships
and the moving rubber cylinders of floats–
heavier than unleaded gasoline,
meant to supervise those who are destitute,
by the land, the sea–
The salt constructs its own castle,
its terra firma in the body of the drinker:
rid of wine, and made sober
by light
and stars and not a curtain for miles.

in favour of movement

can I convince you that
          haphazardness was the game-plan?

even if my dancing nataraja of a soul
          is steamrollered
                    into obedience   into obeisance   into oblivion

it retains a keen resistance
to the caprices of life
in this sole aspect

the laying of my gifts
at the determined keyboard
when in truth there is

          nowhere to write
                    the unbarricaded: the unbridled soul

Act of Faith

Don't pry don't ask to whom I pray
if it changes from day to day,
if the entity is male or female
if I fast and for whom
don't ask, don't ask.

I know there are forms to fill; spaces where I must
write neatly and in caps,
the beliefs I've claimed
dog tags strung tight
around my neck

agnostic, atheist, multi-faith, irreligious, liberal,
gregarious, star-gazer
sun-worshipper
and to top it all
open-minded

yet searching for a word to describe my true religion,
which began one solemn day
when I thought
impermanence could be
invited at will

I wished to be a ribbon of mist trailing in the cold blast of
the stratosphere but found
I'd stayed within
reach of earth; why, I was
still grounded

Drawing breath is an act of faith, one I've embraced
running, jumping, keeping
time, sucking in air, choosing to,
each new day
is religion

Monday to Sunday, just living is an act of faith.

bi-lingual

last night I dreamt that
my tongue split in two
and projected out of my mouth
into the universe

one half spoke English
whilst the other spoke Urdu

my tongues were in parallel
but when I tried to say who I was
I knew the tongues would meet

parallel lines only cross once
never to meet again

I held on to this as *my* cross
thinking I would never be able to move
for fear of losing myself

then I remembered
the Buddhists
and started to
think
vertically

Afterbirth

The last time I saw the sky
it glared at me from outside
the window, enticed me to brave
its witch-white, branch-shadowed storm.

There, I breathed, those deep breaths
taught in relaxation,
learned to lie back
as nature blew on my face and stung.

I waved to each cloud, shook frothy hands
until they melted blue / grey, stirred
up the sun with my brightened heart,
taught it to sing mellow.

Back on the wooden floor at home,
I saw myself in every stain,
felt it press against my skull
with a cold, mothering force.

In Dad's House

I catch myself in ageing mirrors,
hold myself to the light.

I am your child,
but the years have found me

playing a memory for too long.

Lines can be more than a punishment,
more than a branding;

they start my page,
wait for the words to settle like starlings.

There is another life.

Immigrant Irony

There's that sideswipe again, some little Englander telling
me Americans do not understand irony just before claiming

I want my country back. I want mine back too, *this* one
I've lived in since '67; permanent from '76, mirror year with

leaving family behind, also those small-town thugs wanting me
dead and other redneck retributions for a difference that didn't

seem to matter walking home unafraid in Suffolk's midnight
darkened roads, long hair no longer dodging beer cans or

a tree-branch ripped from a neighbour's yard to take a swing.
These obvious violences didn't run to blood in *our* rivers,

but hatred has always been with us, though then tolerances
defined a whole instead of today's long line of fear pasted

on billboards to create rather than cover every growing crack:
so listen to me, little mad Englander, I want *my* country back.

D

You tell yourself you're immune, always, but then D appears, if not exactly out of the shadows then like a river of milk flooding the kitchen. You try laying down towels, try licking D up, fancying yourself a cat, the distant and independent creature disdaining those who clamour for its attention. But the milk rolls from your tongue, continues rising, soaking through the papers on the floor, the books on the chair, drenching your clothing, swirling around your chest, teasing and pressing at your breath. You consider swimming, but D circles your wrists, clamps your ankles together. You'd fight but there's something so soothing about all that milk, warm and sweet, the drug of it, teasing with all that is possible, the breath you retain until your head grows light and you're high with distraction, you're gulping the river down, not to drown in its spectacle but to pull it closer, the sugar of it, you'll give up time and every practicality to keep swallowing until your ears ring like sirens.

precarious

it is exactly noon i am standing

at the black corner of california

and the edge of the world

the bay's chill burnishing my cheeks

it could be any season

people joke

that there *are* four earthquakes

floods fires and construction but we

really know only this one its warm-

bite water weighting the air

or drowning the gutters

making these hills slick as lies why

did people choose to live here

building matchstick victorians

at the place where the ground shoved

its guts toward the sky on this black corner

of california and the edge of life in this never-

one-thing-or-the-other weather up

the slope from our flat with its brick

that will collapse the next time the earth

wrenches   walking is irrelevant   i have

always been here

châtelaine

caretaker of blazes

guard of the auroras and flashes
that streak the backdrops of your fantasy

guide of fragile eyes

herder of torches, ministering to every dream
of implacable darkness

chaperone to transient neon

tender of mirrors and strobes

I'll be the keeper
carefully locking the door
jangling the keys
to warn off thieves

who'd siphon every spark
from this house
where you store
your light

Sabrina of the Severn

Imagine a river.
I want you to be a part of it,
so when the swan dips its head to dive
and drink, you feel a tickle on your tongue.
You'll find me, hair of knotted weeds,
pearl-eyed and silver scaled,
my body sculpted into the mudflats.

The river feeds into the wetlands
where fisherman gather and drink lager
from cool boxes, hooded silhouettes
against the sunrise. As they haul their prized
salmon to their arms for photographs,
you'll find hooks protruding
from the pores of your skin.

We'll bear witness.
The docks brim with bodies
that will fade into old ghosts
with missing teeth.
Their ships retire under grey water
and when the riots begin
we'll break our banks, flood the city streets.

When the body of a woman
is devoured, cut open, spat
back onto the bank, we'll run the river red
and roll her out clean.
Bed of kelp, salt on wounded skin.
Her husband, blood on the cap of his boots
we'll haunt him in his sleep.

Welcome

We're unpacking our bodies
from boxes in my parents'
new rental home.
Home is what we repeat
to ourselves as we take
our internal organs
from the box labelled *fragile.*

I pop my kidneys in the kitchen cupboard
for later use. My mother wraps
her intestines around the curtain rail.
My father paints the walls magnolia
wearing gloves of his own blood.
You would think
we had done this before.

A slice of new moon comes out
for us that first night
and I hear something
under my bed.
There's an old sick heart
in a shoebox, half its tissue
charcoal-black, but still pumping slow,
ba-bum, ba-bum.

I watch the disease spread,
clogging arties, valves and veins
with tar thickness, fast
until the beat
is swallowed whole.

Goldfinch

What part of rubble makes
the architect? In the morning,
orange juice pressed fresh

in memory, tarter, not quite

the sweetenough
of home. This early hour
you wonder

what the hummingbird says

to the goldfinch of its
migration, discovering
that somewhere in the midst

of these past thirty years,

that place was found
mislaid in each
revisitation back to 1988. Now

the church is sinking through

the torn-up streets
of Coyoacan, tree-roots more deliberately
displacing concrete. They

grow too deep. At dusk,

the jacaranda scent infiltrates
colonial walks, their cobbled-ness
delineates peripheries,

and somewhere on the edge

of consciousness,
those untranslatable ridges,
replaced by roads.

Your psychotherapist states

its all a fog, your
confrontation & something else
you were, slips out

unbidden with you

still up at 4 am, still
jet-lagged, from that first time,
when just outside

a bird begins, with me

still wondering what part of you
I lose each day
to another language, another song.

Lullaby

amapola, lindísima amapola

milk tear falling,
falling through,
yo te quiero
in fractured sentences
and memorized wounds
petal-satin soft

igual que ama la flor
in the
even the sun

yo te quiero
indifferent waves

you wait for the fog-fall
save pennies from

Tijuana

it leaves its trace inscribing tombs

amada niña mia
crumbling into red, you too bled
through fingertips
al luz del día
summer
crosses over, is lost to
the other side *la luz del día*
jutting out hard steel spike hard against

amapola, lindísima

a second-hand sale from across

the border in Mexicali, the US wall makes up
the fourth of your home
this is the state transnational trade
you sang to me
un par de ojos negros, cielíto lindo *de contrabando*
before I lost your language to the streets, my 'r's all wrong in Spanish
except when I say three you taught me
counting pebbles the tongue-tide sea kisses the edge
each grain of sand poised in a moment of drowning
inbetween two cities & I'm still waving at you from the bridge we built
when I asked you
don't speak Spanish you sang to me
un par de ojos negros, cielíto lindo *de contrabando*
a pair of tangerine wings flecked
black *ese lunar que tienes*
junto a la boca lips caress as oars divide
an ocean
amada niña mia
no se lo des a nadie
you shut your eyes they searched you
a second time, *amapola*

Deliver

Damp wall against your back,
behind boxes of trainers labelled
MEGA VALUE, you wept.
Sat in a pool of blood, uniform
cast aside, you think about the kid
on the factory line, dream maker
on the breadline. Cord-cutter
turned Stanley knife in your hand
you wonder what yours'll be doing
age seven. Surviving on a pound
a day? No way, this is Britain,
you say out loud. It echoes.

A land of opportunity, progression.
Your neighbours back home envy
your Iphone. They pry and they dream.

Loud shriek in your lap
and you remember
the thing: red, wriggling
around as you wipe him
with paper towels, wrap
his sumo wrestler-like body:
the warehouse chills to the bone.
He cries and cries as you pull up
your jeans, thighs sticky
from blood, you shiver
as you look back one last time.
Babies bring hope, they say.

You've got to finish the shift
You've got to finish the shift
You've got to finish

Hopscotch

Plastic bag, six bread rolls
or five, forward and back.

Father walking head-down in brown
on stones like hopscotch.

Back from the store, ten Forints a roll
six rolls five rolls father fading out. Fading in.

Plastic rustles corduroy flaps
rusty, red concrete towers above, shielding

the wrong side. Gusty wind blows
from the west. I rummage for keys, hear

plastic, corduroy, an image in my head.
I look back

a mirage
on stones
like hopscotch.
Flapping corduroy.
Rustling plastic.
Flapping.
Rustling.
Fading.

Autumn leaves

I'm ashamed the sound of feet on autumn leaves
Reminds me of you eating honey flakes.

Your teeth the feet
that trample yellow, red, brown.
Trees shed their gown,
the frost draws near.

Under my kitchen window,
one falls on the garden chair.
I close my eyes and picture
elms in the park.

A handful in your fist
you laughed and threw them in the air.
I looked up at the colours, morning dew,
one stuck in my hair

Our feet were soon bare
toes poking through a pile
I told you they're called 'avar'
language teacher-me made you smile.

My garden chair is white
with a pillow made of leaves, red, wet.
I soak the flakes in my bowl
and forget, forget, forget.

Displacement

A few days after I arrived I got my period.
A small, round patch on the white crotch
of my underwear, as violet and
delicate as a peach pit, which always
rises to meet teeth. Salty heat, a dust cake
of air curling in, underneath my clothes.
Wearing clothes is like being naked here.
Being naked here is like being submerged.

I have western hips.
I am uprooted in China,
my tendrils shivering skywards,
a pathetic display of wordless feeling,
because I can ask for yoghurt drink
and where the bathroom is and powder
for sweat rash but cannot tell you how
coming back here is almost like grief.
My own name – mixed blood – is cloth
soaking up iron and zinc. I squat down
over the toilet with my hand bunched
in my skirt and do not know why
I was born.

China is a dream that slips away
in Glasgow. I come close
to comprehending it
in my peripheral vision,
but it stings my eyes to look
right at it. I think that I am
sometimes still a fetus,
everything and nothing,
waiting to be translated into
air, light, a recognisable shape.

Chinglish

The language of love.
God, mama, just your
sheng yin rang wo de xin
open like a loose dumpling.
The warmth of the pork steam,
billowing up to my chin.
I didn't realise chives and
jiu cai were the same thing.
The way pin yin rounds out
meaning for me, plucks chords
out of conversation like a dancer,
tiao lai tiao qu. Where I miss steps
you make up for it. Yong ying wen
ze me shuo? Just like this.

Ah Kong held our family together

Waking in the black hours,
he sliced grooves
into tree every 20 seconds,
then cycled miles from estate
to morning shift-school.
While the trees yielded milky latex,
he tended these other saplings.
Tapping, he guided students'
calligraphy forming like treelace.

Then sun warmed everything.
Sap congealed in smallholder's cups,
white lumps for cents, salt, rice.
Days were long and still
his children couldn't eat until full.
An elastic band draws descendants
together. Monsoon comes,
mosquitos swarming
the rubbertapper's oil-lit lamp.

Bakkwa

because we could never be home
for Chinese New Year   aunts gift
sticky squares of pork   box big
enough for eighteen airborne hours

because sesame   fish sauce
five spice heats   dídí's breath
and chilli coats   my tongue
because I am thirteen   and he's ten

because we can't eat it all
want something for the days ahead
because we lie   declare nothing at customs
we are stopped

My ghosts rattle

too scaly for politeness, drooling
as I load up the altar table;
intractable with hunger, mouths
intent as candles, throats
tapering like tattoo needles.
The priest inscribes, a woman is no longer
a pitaya, fruit without kernel.

Ah Jè interprets the kau cim:
sa: chick yiyap-ik   kin-raw-bones.
I am dried joss, coils of which
my unhatched son ignites
outside the temple with his daughters.
Black against the sun, umbrellas
shade skins from dispersing ash.

Komodo sister, you are brooding
kindness below the soil.
Clutches of round words
incubate in sand-silence,
their fetches monitored.
Forking smoke, I intone
the 21 uses of dragon eggs.

از شهریکه من آمده‌ام

در اکثر نقاط دنیا معمولاً چهار فصل است
از شهریکه من آمده‌ام،همیشه زمستان است
سرما و تند باد و طوفانی و آتشفشان
در اکثر نقاط جهان فقط برف و باران میبارد
اما از شهریکه من آمده‌ام
آسمان‌اش پر از رعد و برق است
در دیگر مناطق جهان انسان‌ها و پرندگان
فقط دو دست و دو پا دارند
اما انسان‌ها و پرندگان سرزمین ما
بعضی‌شان فقط یک دست و یا یک پا دارند و
بعضی‌شان هیچ دست و پای ندارند
آتش جنگ دست و پا و پر و بال‌شان
یا شکسته یا کاملاً قطع کرده
در قلب انسان‌های دیگر مناطق جهان خون در جریان است
اما در رگهای بدن انسان‌های سرزمین ما آتش شعله‌ور است
مردمان اکثر نقاط جهان سه وقت غذا مصرف می‌نمایند
اما مردمان سرزمین ما بجای غذا آه و حسرت و غم و اندوه
ما بی‌گناهان مجرم و مجرمان بی‌گناه‌ایم
تعداد از مردمان ما اگر فرصت فرار به نقاط امن از جهان را یافته
که در صلح و آرامش به سر برند
حاکمان آن سرزمین بر ما پوزخند می‌زنند
گویند ما لیاقت زیستن در صلح و امنیت را نداریم
گویند بروید ترک ما کنید
بعضی‌شان بر ما می‌خندند
رفتار ما برای‌شان غیر معمولی
و مشکوک است
از شرایط جنگ و خشونت متاثریم
فکر می‌کنند ما از سیاره‌ای دیگر آمده‌ایم

The City I Come From

Every part of the world
has its seasons
but in the city I come from
it is always winter
with icy winds, volcanic storms

There is snow and rain
in other parts of the world
But in the city I come from
The sky is always
heavy with thunder

In other places
people have two legs
and the birds have two wings
but in the city I come from
some people have one leg, some have none

Even some of the birds have
only one wing
The never-ending war
has cut off their legs
burnt their wings

In other countries people's hearts
pump blood
but in my country
instead of blood
our veins run with fire

Most people, they say
have meals three times a day
but instead of food and water
our people feed on
bitterness and sorrow

Tr. James Attlee

We are innocent, but guilty
we are guilty, yet innocent

Now some of us
have had the chance
to escape
to other parts of the world
where there is peace and safety

But the rulers of these lands play a joke on us
They think we don't deserve to live
in peace and prosperity
they are trying to push us out,
telling us to go away

Some people laugh at us
to them we look
strange, suspicious
because we have no smile on our lips
no confidence

To them
we look
like people
from another
planet

کاروان

کاروان شهر تاراج گشته‌ایم
خسته و آواره و گمراه استیم
کوله بار رنج تاریخ ایم به پشت
ساربان کشته، فانوس مرده‌ایم
برگ پاییزی‌ایم وتندباد خزان
چو غزال نوزاد ز مادر مانده‌ایم
طعمه‌ای گرگان در وقت اذان
هم تگرگ و هم باد و هم پلنگ
پا برهنه، دست شکسته راه تنگ
روی به سوی آسمان کردم غریید
سوی چشمه رفتم و سیلاب گشت
تا پناه بردم بغاری
افعی باز کرد دهان
همچنان از تشنگی داشتم هلاک
جرعه‌ای آبی ز ساقی خواستم
سرکشیدم جام را بیهوش شدم
بعد صد سال آمدم دیگر به حال
تا نگاه کردم خودم در آیینه
گرچه من شیری ژیان آسیا
گربه پیری ضعیفی یافتم

Caravan

We are the caravan
that has left the looted city
we are travelling
but we have lost our way

The burden on our backs
is the powerful weight of history
the leader of our caravan has died
and the lantern that guided us has gone out

We are like autumn leaves
scattered by the wind—
We are the new born fawns of the gazelle
whose mother has gone

When the muezzin calls
in the early morning darkness
we are food for the wolves

The wind
besieges us with snowdrifts
and we are circled by tigers

Our hands and our legs are broken
and the way ahead is narrow
We look to the sky for God's help
but the only answer comes in a bolt of lightning

I went to the mountain spring to drink
but it had become a torrent
I went to find shelter in a cave
but inside was coiled a cobra

I was near death from thirst
I begged for a drink of water from the waiter

I drank all his glasses dry
and fell to the ground, unconscious

After one hundred years
I awoke
and when I looked in the mirror

Instead of a strong
mountain lion
I saw an old, weak cat

Ekta-chrome

I.

man takes a woman
on a wedding trip
before I was born

last look upon home,
a café on the village square,
the field, its harvest of exile

pellucid Pelasgia
partial coinage
of a man-made image

or something like this
tangible language, this audible curve,
this emotionese

he left me
this ring
of partial glimpses

II.

the way I see it
I was left
to translate him

lift his disembodied eye
to my eye, find no archive of anecdota
but shed and shadow

self recognition in this Cézannesque
square: a basket of fruit, sun-dappled wall--
I set my sepia-toned pastorals

against his transparency: modern markers of industry,
café tray, glass-bottled sodas, metal ashcan
are what I sought to leave out

III.

he left me
this ring
of partial glimpses

the way I see it
I was left
to translate him

"apple, o apple of my eye,"
he called me
matia mou, you who are my eyes--

why Ekta-chrome? I pressed him,
paper is ephemeral, he thought
slide film is better, it'll last

last, last, little pools of memory
until this cold water
shall trickle
                over

Losing myself

I waited next to the neon lights
written in cryptic Chinese characters.

Tap, tap, on the window pane
clouded in humid condensation.

But, still your smile
shone through the opaque glass.

I opened my door, closed my door
and followed you across the street.

Takero like *te queiro*: I love you.
It's how you introduced yourself.

Inside your house, you asked me
to undress and follow you once more.

We went to your washroom,
where you preceeded to wash my body.

You studied the shape of my round bottom,
told me what you planned to do to it.

Your tongue explored me, and for a moment,
I wondered what I tasted like.

You filled my body with all of you,
taught me how two bodies move as one.

I wondered if it were possible,
for a body to be broken in this way.

When I left your place,
I could not be certain that I was the same.

I opened my door, closed my door,
rolled down the window to defog the car.

I looked up at the neon sign,
and drew in the air, let it fill my body.

Exhaling, as both the old man,
and the one about to drive away.

32 teeth

32 teeth. I couldn't name them all. Molars. Babies. Wisdom teeth… Do they bring me wisdom? I'm looking at her (who really is everyone). And, I smile. Sonreír. Yo sonrío. Smiling through it all: that uncomfortable feeling. Smiling through the need to run. Smiling politely. Smiling correctly. Not trying to turn political. 32 teeth, but I couldn't name them all for you. Even if I wanted to. Couldn't neatly categorise those pearly whites. She keeps talking and I've stoped listening. But still I smile con una sonrisa pequeña. Smiling with 32 teeth and nodding. My smile is my only defence. My smile is insincere.

The Holy Land

The lullabies in Gaza are sung in bombs,
houses that rock little babies to sleep.

The blood that spills flows next to the Jordan,
the sea overflowing with tears that mothers weep.

We are the Dead Sea,
but we are not floating.

We are helplessly sinking deep.

Sweet Love

If I steal a few kisses
baubles of sweet love
pressed to my lips
gifted from hers -

must I do it behind closed doors
in hidden rooms and secret hidings
of feelings long kept buried
for safe keeping

Can I love her the way I did my others
and bring her home, for she already lives there
and hold her hand as though they were woven

Palms closely, tightly, embraced together
keeping this fragile heart of mine
warm and longed for

Yearning forever.

At Ramsis Station

When the news broke of a fire in Ramsis, it was as though I could feel its very flames engulfing my heart.

I first thought of you and of the grand walls of the station, that housed our big smiles and a warm embrace after days apart. I thought of how its platforms delayed the trains, almost as if to give us some extra time for more kisses and long goodbyes.

Then, I thought of the girl who sat next to me. She was studying for exams that she travels three hours to sit. How she told me about her dreams, as I tested her on questions I didn't know the answers to.

I then thought of the father standing on the platform, holding his little daughter. How they both waved profusely, as his wife got settled into her seat – as they ran and ran alongside the train, until they could no longer keep up.

I thought of the elderly woman, who jumped the tracks with kilos of flour balanced on her head. She was about my grandmother's age, working in the blistering heat - trying to make a living for her children. While I was on my way back to Alexandria, to spend what I didn't know would be my grandmother's last days.

I thought of the single mother I had spotted on my morning train, with two children and not a single train ticket. How the man sitting next to me paid for three, just so she could make her journey.

I thought of my friend, John and of the first time we met – how he offered me a seat by his bookshop. How he charged my phone on a night when my train got delayed, and I was waiting alone. He continued to offer me a seat every time I went back to Cairo and gifted me a book to remember him by.

As I waited for my last train that summer, all the others stared and stared at the sight of young love on Cairo's platform. John gave me a tissue to wipe my tears and reminded me of the rarity in having a love that hurts to leave behind. Little did we both know that I was leaving it behind on that platform for good.

I thought of the last time I was at Ramsis. How I was no longer leaving behind love, but a friendship that grew out of it.

I thought of all these people.

If they got a chance to say goodbye.
If they were on their way to say hello.

Itchy feet

They say that when you're pregnant, your sense of smell changes
And though I know there's no baby, there is *something*
Taken root inside me, furling and unfurling,
Too green and lively to be birthed in Spain.

All the old places have changed their scents.
The wooden bridge from la Lleona to Jutjats smells like
Clinker-built boats stuck in Brightlingsea creek, cracks filled with black mud and sunshine.
The cobbles in Plaça del Vi rattle under my feet like King's Parade

And the moon is a high silver five pence piece. All my money's out of date.
Storm clouds pile up like grey concrete lumps of London
And there's rain in the wind. Every time an aeroplane goes overhead
I watch it out of sight, in case it touches down for me.

My feet itch. My lust wanders. Yesterday I opened the window
and the afternoon smelled like Greece;
garlic frying in a pan smells like Austria.
That open door is wafting out the scent of Christchurch. Ice cream tastes like August in Lucerne.

Like Mary Poppins I can feel it's time to go;
The wind has changed its perfume, and my compass swings around.
I can't sit still. So I book another flight,
And wonder if I ever will.

Visiting

Before they come, I tidy myself away
Into cupboards and behind closed doors.
Ironing my creases out of seats and sofas,
I dust away my fingerprints and mop the floor,
Polish the glass so as to leave no ripples
Of my voice. I catch my own eyes in the mirror
And deposit them safely in the box where we keep
Spare keys and sets of dice.
I air out the air that I have breathed
And run the taps that I have drunk from, clean.
I hang up my memories again,
Just as they were, in the correct locations.
I wash my face, check for damp and condensation.
Lock the door. Wipe my footprints from the mat.

Calling Moscow

The same moon that shines down on me
Is breaking ice in the Moscow sky.
Even aeroplanes don't buzz that high,
Or soar that far across the sea.
I know exactly where you'll be.
It's wintertime, four hours ahead,
So you'll be curled in that dim cramped room
Watching *Kung Fu Panda*, or *Life of Brian*,
Or anything from a place or time when
We were innocent of Moscow things –
Moscow things, like microphones hidden in plastic rocks
And anti-tank installations disguised as giant flowerpots.
I'm not going to call you.
I hate the way your voice is jointed up into little, frozen, static shocks
And when the line goes dead, that *click-clickclickclick-click*
Like insects swarming up the side of the house.
There's a tapeworm living in your answerphone machine did you know?
Of course you knew.
I am back in England now.
I am safe, I am where we're all supposed to be.
The moon shines down on Moscow and finds no trace of me.
But still if strange men follow me
I don't run, or scream, or threaten them
But turn and ask:
And when they seem confused I let them pass.
I'm waiting for one of them to stop, and pull a frozen tapeworm from between his teeth
And then I'll know the flowerpots have been smashed.
And then I'll know you're never coming back.

Authors

Yvonne Litschel

Yvonne Litschel is a poet and artist currently between London and the Fens. She has published three solo pamphlets, Moth Dust (Sampson Low), Immurement (Broken Sleep Books) and ræfs (Ghost City Press), and has been featured in two Sidekick Books anthologies. In 2019 she placed second in the Streetcake Experimental Writing Prize for poetry. At present she is studying MA Publishing at University of the Arts London.yvonnelitschel.com @yvlitschel

Lou Sarabadzic

Lou Sarabadzic is a French bilingual writer based in Warwickshire. She has published two poetry collections in French: *Ensemble* and *Portrait du bon goût en individu ma foi plutôt aimable*. You can find her on Twitter @lousarabadzic, or visit her website, www.lousarabadzic.com. You can read more about the form for Acrostiche Brivadois here: https://www.oulipo.net/fr/contraintes/acrostiche-brivadois

Amy Evans Bauer

Amy Evans Bauer is an Anglo-Austrian Kiwi poet based in London. *and umbels.* (Jonathan Williams Chapbooks prize, 2020) and *PASS PORT* (Shearsman, 2018) form the transcript of her at-sea, cross-border installation *SOUND((ING))S*. Her poetry features in *Chicago Review* and *Dear World and Everyone In It* (Bloodaxe, 2013), and elsewhere.

'Lacrimosa' by was commissioned in 2017 as part of the Polish Government's 'The Year of Joseph Conrad' celebrations, and performed at the National Poetry Library for Conrad's 160th birthday, organised by Robert Hampson and Agnieszka Studzinska. Text from 'What Teargas is For' copyright © Sean Bonney, and used with the author's permission.

Yvette Siegert

Yvette Siegert is a Latinx poet born in Los Angeles to immigrants from Colombia and El Salvador. A CantoMundo Fellow, she is winner of the Lord Alfred Douglas Prize and the Best Translated Book Award and was recently shortlisted for the Rebecca Swift Foundation's Women Poets Prize. She is currently reading for a DPhil in Spanish-American literature at Merton College, Oxford.

California Roll first appeared in *The Scores* (June 2020), and Vitreous was first published by *the Oxford Review of Books* (2019).

Gustavo Barahona-López

Gustavo Barahona-López is a poet and educator from Richmond, California. In his writing, Barahona-López draws from his experience growing up in a Mexican immigrant household. His micro-chapbook *Where Will the Children Play?* is part of the Ghost City Press 2020 Summer Series. A VONA alumn, Barahona-López's work can be found or is forthcoming in Glass' Poets Resist, Cosmonauts Avenue, The Acentos Review, Apogee Journal, Hayden's Ferry Review, among other publications.

Emma Filtness

Emma Filtness is a poet and lecturer in Creative Writing at Brunel University London. Her poetry recently featured in Poem Atlas and Mellom Press visual poetry exhibitions. Emma finds inspiration in nature and the dark feminineTwitter:
@em_filtness Instagram: @cultofflora

Arielle Jasiewicz-Gill

Arielle Jasiewicz-Gill is a freelance writer based in the South East of England who is currently studying for a master's in Medieval Studies at the University of Oxford. At present, she also runs an online blog where she self-publishes a selection of her creative writing and thought pieces.

Mizzy Hussain

Mizzy Hussain was born in East Lancashire, where she lived throughout her childhood, apart from two early years in Pakistan. When she was 9 years old she knew she wanted to be an 'author'. A short creative non-fiction course at Birkbeck College, London (1993/4) led to the publication of her first short story, published in an anthology 'How Maxine Learned To Love Her Legs' (Aurora Metro Press, 1995). She has an MSc in Creative Writing from the University of Edinburgh (2005) and is currently resident in Scotland where she identifies herself as a Lancastrian-in-Exile.

Judith Kingston

Judith Kingston is a Dutch writer living in the UK. Her poetry has appeared in a number of magazines including Barren Magazine, Ghost City Press, Riggwelter and Kissing Dynamite. Her micro-chapbook *Mother is the Name for God* was published by Ghost City Press in 2020.

Isabelle Baafi

Isabelle Baafi is a writer and poet from London. She was the winner of the 2019 Vincent Cooper Literary Prize, and was shortlisted for the 2019 Oxford Brookes International Poetry Competition. Her debut pamphlet, *Ripe,* was recently published by ignitionpress.

Iulia David

Iulia David is a Romanian-born poet living in London. Her poetry appears in various magazines including Poetry Ireland Review, The Scores, Magma, The Rialto, and Under the Radar. You can read more of her work on www.fox.horse

George Ttoouli

George Ttoouli is a writer and teacher based in Coventry. His latest collection of poetry is *from Animal Illicit* (Broken Sleep Books, 2020).

Cristina Lai

Cristina Lai is an Asian-American woman with a long family history of trying to find a place to call home. She is a writer and an engineer and can be found at @cristinabridget across the internet.

Arturo Desimone

Arturo Desimone, Arubian-Argentinian writer and visual artist, born 1984 on the island Aruba which he inhabited until the age of 22, when he emigrated to the Netherlands. He later relocated to Argentina while working on projects related to his Argentinean family background. Desimone's articles, poetry and fiction pieces previously appeared in CounterPunch, Círculo de Poesía (Spanish) Island, the Drunken Boat, The Missing Slate, EuropeNow, the Writers Resist anthology, Al Araby Al Jadeed (Arabic) and New Orleans Review. He performed at the most recent edition of the international poetry festival of Granada, Nicaragua. Two collections of poetry and visual art recently appeared in the UK and in Argentina: " Mare Nostrum / Costa Nostra " (Hesterglock Press, 2019) and "Ouafa and Thawra: About a Lover from Tunisia" appeared in the UK and throughout Africa and in bilingual editions as La Amada de Túnez in his second homeland Argentina in 2020

Kavita A. Jindal

Kavita A. Jindal is the author of the novel *Manual For A Decent Life*, which won the Brighthorse Prize, and of two slim volumes of poetry: *Patina* and *Raincheck Renewed*. She was born and raised in India and became a British citizen twenty-five years ago. www.kavitajindal.com

in favour of movement - First published in Home Thoughts, Cyberwit, 2017. Act of Faith - First published in Cha literary journal, Issue 1, 2007

Zah Rasul

Zah's poetry and short stories have appeared in a number of small press publications including The Los Angeles Review. Zah lives and work in London and runs a creative writing class in Walthamstow.

K. S. Moore

K. S. Moore is a Welsh poet, based in Ireland. Her poetry has recently appeared in New Welsh Review, Atlanta Review and Verity La. She blogs at ksmoore.com.

Mike Ferguson

Mike Ferguson is an American permanently resident in the UK.

Michelle Penn

Michelle Penn's debut pamphlet, *Self-Portrait as a diviner, failing*, was published in 2018 (Paper Swans Press). She's from a Lithuanian/South African/American family and lives in London.

D first appeared in B O D Y and Precarious first appeared in NOON: Solstice Shorts Festival 2018 (Arachne Press).

Taylor Edmonds

Taylor Edmonds is a poet & performer from South Wales. She has an MA in Creative Writing from Cardiff University. Her work explores womanhood, magic & connection.

Maia Elsner

Maia Elsner grew up between Oxford and Mexico City. Her poems have been published in Magma, Stand, Brittle Star, and Blackbox Manifold, among others. She was shortlisted for the 2019 White Review's Poet's Prize and the 2020 Mairtín Crawford Prize in Poetry, and was commended for the 2020 Geoff Stevens Memorial Prize.

Nóra Blascsók

Nora Blascsok writes poetry and lives by the sea. She grew up in Budapest and moved to the UK when she was 21. You can find her poems online in Streetcake Magazine, Cypress Poetry, Pink Plastic House and some other places.

Lady Red Ego

Lady Red Ego is a Chinese/British lesbian poet and writer concerned with intimacies. Her first pamphlet, *The Red Ego,* was published last year with Wild Pressed Books and her second pamphlet, *Natural Sugars,* was published this year by Broken Sleep Books. Her work has also featured in two videos on BBC The Social.

L. Kiew

A chinese-malaysian living in London, L Kiew earns her living as an accountant. Her debut pamphlet *The Unquiet* came out with Offord Road Books in 2019.

Hasan Bamyani

Hasan Bamyani is the author of the collection *Lyla and Majnoon* published by Exiled Writers Ink in 2008 and translated by Carole Angier and had poems included in *The Story of My Life: Refugee Writing in Oxford*, published by The Charlbury Press, 2005. His poem Darde Dell, translated by James Attlee, was published by the Oxford Review of Books in 2019.

James Attlee

James Attlee is the author of Isolarion: A Different Oxford Journey (2007/2020), Guernica: Painting the End of the World (2017) and Under the Rainbow: Voices from the First Lockdown (2021), among other titles

Vasiliki Katsarou

Vasiliki Katsarou is a Greek and US citizen who grew up in Jack Kerouac's hometown of Lowell, Massachusetts and later moved to Paris, France. She is the author of the poetry collection, *Memento Tsunami*, and a chapbook *Three Sea Stones*. She currently lives in Hunterdon County, New Jersey.

The poem "Ekta-chrome" was first published last year in Ergon: Greek/American Arts and Letters

Andrés N. Ordorica

Andrés N Ordorica is an Edinburgh-based queer Latinx writer who creates characters who are from neither here nor there (ni de aquí, ni de allá).

Meriem Ahmed

Meriem Ahmed is an Irish/Egyptian poet and writer. 'Truth Be Told' is her first poetry collection which she penned at nineteen, releasing it three years following.

Ahmed values most the vulnerability in her words and believes it to be the most crucial aspect in her work. Through it, she hopes that her dedication to authentic story-telling acts as a reminder to her readers that they are never alone in the world, should they ever feel like it.

Corrina Keefe

Corinna Keefe is a freelance writer who has lived and worked in ten different countries

LAY OUT YOUR UNREST

Lightning Source UK Ltd.
Milton Keynes UK
UKHW020706090122
396826UK00009B/457